I am top cat.

Am I top cat?

I am! I am!

I am top cat.

Am I top cat?

I am! I am!

7

Am I top cat?

Tom got a pot.

1

Pam got a pot.

Sam got a pot.

3

Pat, pat, pat!

Tom

A cat

Tap, tap, tap!
Tap, tap, tap!

Tom got a mop!

Bob is a bug.

Bob Bug has a mum. His mum is big.

Bob has a dad. His dad is fit.

Bob has a cup. It has a lid.

Bob has a cot. His cot has a rug.

5

6

7

Bob Bug has a hug.

8

Dig, dig, dig!
Tim and his dog had fun.

Dig, dig, dig!
Tim dug up a lot of mud.

Dig, dig, dig!
His dog dug up a rag.

3

Dig, dig, dig!
Tim dug up a bus.

Dig, dig, dig!
A lid!

5

Dig, dig, dig!
A big tin!

And in it. . .

lots of bugs!

1

Zak did not sit. Zak ran.

3

Zak ran in the fog.
A red van hit him.

Jen and Zak went to the vet.

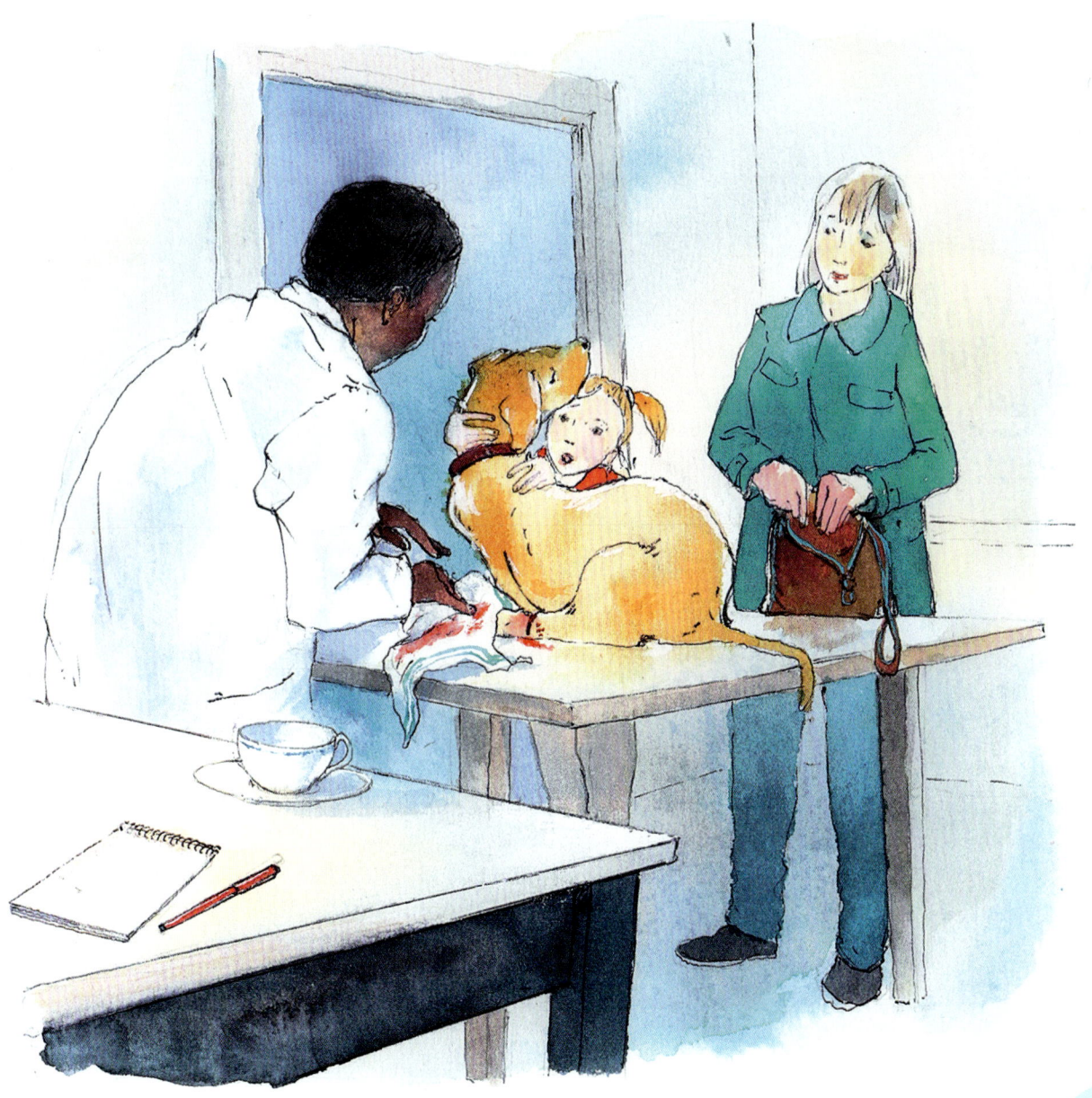

Zak had a bad cut. He had to get a jab.

Will Zak get better?

7

Zak did get better.

wag wag wag

Mum Bug has a red bag.
The bag has a zip.

Mum can fit a pen in her bag.

Mum can fit a pen and
a fan in her bag.

Mum can fit a pen and
a fan and
a bun in her bag.

Mum can fit a pen and
a fan and
a bun and
a pot of jam in her bag.

Mum has a hole in her bag!

The pen and
the fan and
the bun and
the jam get wet.

Mum Bug gets a big bag.

Bob Bug was in his cot.

"Get up, Bob," said Dad.

But Bob did not get up.
"I am hot!" he said.

3

"Bob is sick!" said Mum. "Quick! I will ring Doctor Duck."

"Mum is a fusspot," said Dad.

Mum Bug rang Doctor Duck.

"Come quick!" she said.
"Bob is sick!"

"Quack, quack!" said Doctor Duck. He got his box of pills.

"I will mix this pill up with some milk," he said.

"Sip this," said Doctor Duck to Bob Bug.

"Yuk," said Bob, but he had
a sip.

"Quack, quack!" said
Doctor Duck.

"I will come back in six days."

When Doctor Duck came back,
Bob was hopping and singing.

But Dad Bug was in bed.
"I am hot! I am sick!" he said.

"Bad luck, Dad," said Mum.
"Dad is a fusspot!" said Bob.

Dad is a singer.

He sings all day long.

Song,   after song,

after song,    after song!

3

He sings to the cat and
he sings to the dog.

4

He sings in the sun

and he sings in the fog.

He sings in the shops

and he sings in the shed.

He sings in the bus

and he sings in his bed.

He sings when he's fishing.

He sings when he jogs.

He sings when he's digging

and chopping up logs.

Mum tells Dad off.
"I'm fed up with that song."

Mum *never* sings ...

but she *hums* all day long!

This is Ron Rabbit.

Ron has a job in a fish and chip shop.

2

4

5

6

9

11

14

15

16

This is Mr Chan's shop.

Mr Chan sells pens, pads and maps.

Tim is in Mr Chan's shop.

4

This is Miss Thin's shop.

Miss Thin sells eggs, nuts and carrots.

Tim is in Miss Thin's shop.

9

This is Mrs Ship's shop.

Mrs Ship sells jugs, shells and chess sets.

Tim is in Mrs Ship's shop.

14

15

This is Tim's rabbit!

2

3

5

9

10

11

Brrrrrrrrrr!

Yes!
The bell!

12

Miss Hill gets on the bus.

Miss Hill gets off the bus.

15

16

Kim has a cat. Jim has a dog.

But Viv has an odd pet.

It is a zog! Not a cat, not a dog, but a zog!

The zog is fat. It has ten red legs.

It can run and hop.

It can sit and beg.

The zog has lots of eggs!

The zog sits on the eggs.
It sits and sits.

Tap, tap, tap!
Tap, tap, tap!

Lots of zogs!

12

13

Now Kim has a cat and a zog.

Jim has a dog and a zog.

15

And Viv has ten zogs!